CREATING
A HERB
GARDEN

CREATING
A HERB
GARDEN

ANTHONY GARDINER

SUNBURST BOOKS

This edition published 1996 by
Sunburst Books
Kiln House, 210 New Kings Road
London SW6 4NZ

ISBN 1 85778 250 X

Publisher's Note
Neither the Publisher nor the Author take any responsibility for the implementation of
any recommendations, ideas or techniques expressed or described in this book. Any use
to which the recommendations, ideas and techniques are put is at the Reader's sole decision and risk.

Printed and bound in China

CONTENTS

Herb Style and Design

Deciding on the right style for your herb garden depends largely on your individual needs. The many uses herbs can be put to can make this choice for you. There are culinary, medicinal, traditional, formal, aromatic and even informal layouts. You can even go for a historical garden or plant to a theme, such as a paradise, Shakespearean or butterfly garden. The theme, or use, usually dictates the style, and from there you can develop your ideas and add other features.

Herb gardens are never dull. Too often the considered opinion is that because many herbs have a short flowering time and die down in the winter, then a herb garden is of limited interest. This merely shows lack of imagination. The fact that herb gardens have been cultivated since early times clearly demonstrates their versatility and durability.

Not everyone has a garden, but many flat-dwellers have either a balcony or a window sill. Very small gardens often have paved areas for sitting out, with not much room for anything other than a table and chairs. Yet such spaces can be utilised to best effect with moveable pots and hanging baskets, as well as the ever popular windowbox. Herbs can be grown quite successfully this way, even though they never reach their full potential, and an attractive and useful display can be achieved for quite a small outlay.

The kitchen herb garden

When most people think of herbs they think of cooking. The 'pot herbs' were an essential part of flavouring in the days when meats were tasteless and grey: they helped to break down fats and acted as digestives. Nowadays herbs have an infinite number of uses in the kitchen, and so the culinary herb garden where herbs can be gathered fresh is a must for any cook.

A sunny site as near to the kitchen as possible is the ideal location. It doesn't need to be a large garden, but it does need to contain those plants that you most like to use. Having chosen the site, decide upon the shape and size; for example, whether it should be round or square-shaped. Very often herbs are planted among the vegetables as companion plants, and utilise the natural shade and rows in between the vegetables. Tall perennials must be allowed plenty of room and placed so they don't mask the lower growing varieties. This may seem obvious, but it is surprising how many, in the desire to plant out quickly, forget this cardinal rule.

Right: This small front garden with formal brick design is almost obscured by perennial evergreen herbs planted singly in the spaces.

In medieval times herbs were planted in strips. This still works well if you are cutting on a regular basis and in large quantities. For the everyday family kitchen a neatly divided bed with chequerboard paving or bricks will compartmentalise your herbs and contain them, and at the same time create an attractive display. Pots of herbs can be moved into sunny positions on terraces, and windowboxes can contain a small selection for use when the needs are minimal.

If you want to grow herbs indoors it is best to keep them out of the kitchen, or at least away from the cooker, as the grease in the air clogs up the pores in the leaves. An ideal place for indoor herbs is in an airy room or conservatory.

The potager style garden is the most versatile of all kitchen gardens with herbs and vegetables grown in individual beds within a very formal setting. The most famous is at Villandry in France. At Villandry there are weeping roses at the corners of rectangular beds, like gardeners tending each plot. The beds are edged with box or wall germander, and plants are displayed in an ornamental way.

Another type of kitchen garden is the herb spiral. This is a helter-skelter shape using old bricks to create a spiral bed. It creates ideal conditions for different herbs in as small a space as possible. Herbs such as rosemary that need dry soil can be grown at the top, and moisture-lovers such as chives and garlic are grown at the bottom of the 'slide'. The overall effect is of an early fortification in miniature, overgrown with herbs.

A number of kitchen herbs are annuals, so allow for spaces among the perennials to grow these. The gaps are not so obvious then in the winter months. Paths from the kitchen to the herbs are essential, and if the beds are quite deep a stepping stone or two helps to get close to plants for cutting.

The medicinal herb garden

Medicinal herb gardens are also known as physic gardens or apothecary gardens. The traditional physic garden has evolved from the monastic infirmary garden which was carefully laid out with easily identifiable herbs grown in separate beds within an enclosed courtyard or fenced surround. Such a herb garden had to provide all the healing plants necessary for the care of the sick both within and without the monastery walls. The hospital was sited at the perimeter of the monastic buildings and apart from it, in order to be able to isolate the contagious and terminally sick.

What is little known is that lay women and religious women worked together with the monks in these hospitals, in spite of the closed nature of many of these orders.

At Magdalen College Oxford, a botanical garden was founded in 1621 as part of the school of medicine. Just over 50 years later, in 1674, the Society of Apothecaries in London established the Chelsea Physic Garden, which exists to this day as a centre for study and research into medicinal plants. These gardens, still in existence, have geometrically-ordered layouts, and all plants are labelled so they can be clearly identified.

A number of medicinal plants are shade-lovers, and it is as well to take this into account when planning the position of your herbs. The term *officinalis* denotes medicinal properties, and the fact that the plant has been used traditionally in medicine.

Not all herbs are safe to eat, and some have quite adverse effects on the system, so although the leaf of comfrey is similar to the leaf of foxglove, the actions are quite different. It is a very good idea to keep these two well apart. Decide early on whether or not you are going to grow poisonous plants, and be aware that children are often attracted to the fruit of plants such as deadly nightshade and mandrake.

There is a mystical quality to medicinal gardens in which the plants that are grown have been associated with either magical or spiritual properties, depending on the age in which they were used. Many of the so-called 'magic' herbs have been given Christian names associated with saints and the Virgin Mary - for example, lady's mantle, St John's wort and angelica.

It is a good idea to design beds for the medicinal garden that relate to those parts of the body the herbs can treat. Or you can label beds according to the various ailments they treat. And if you planned a 'Culpeper' garden you might arrange beds according to the signs of the zodiac. Whatever you decide, the most important thing to do during the planning and planting stage is to do your research thoroughly and label every plant clearly. Then you can set about a serious botanical study of your private physic garden.

Do not be disheartened by the rather clinical construction of the medicinal herb garden; remember it is the healing properties of these plants rather than their aesthetic properties that matter.

Below: A wall makes a perfect feature for a scented garden as it reflects the heat and retains the scent of aromatic and fragrant plants.

The aromatic garden

The scented garden is the most romantic of herb gardens. This is a place that invites you to relax and indulge your senses. Old-fashioned roses, banks of thyme, sweet bergamot, pinks – they all conjure up the image of the aromatic garden.

Ideally, the scented herb garden should be quite small, with a seat or grassy bank as its focal point. Always place your seat where the prevailing wind can waft the scents towards you. Surround the garden with sweet-smelling hedges of rosemary, southernwood or lavender. A wattle fence can act as a windbreak on which you can grow honeysuckle or wild roses. It is essential to enclose the garden to retain the scent. Arbours covered with jasmine or hops will contain the scents around your seat.

Grow ground cover herbs that like to be trodden on, such as pennyroyal, creeping thymes and chamomile. These release their scent when crushed, while others such as winter savory, when planted at the edges of paths, will release their scent when you brush past them. The grey feathery forms of the artemisias invite you to touch them as you pass, and enjoy their unique perfume.

At different times of the year different scents dominate. Early in the summer the subtle scents of the apothecary rose fill the air with soft scent. Later the pinks hit your senses with a rush. Not all scents delight everyone. An aromatic garden is a very subjective garden; what may appeal to one person may be offensive to another, so choose your plants with care and try to experience the pungent aroma of herbs such as santolina when they are in flower, and before you begin to plant them out.

The aromatic garden also depends on colour and form, as it is equally appealing to the eye. Fortunately most herbs have soft pastel colours and the dark green foliage can be mixed with greys and golds. The flowers attract bees, and on a hot summer day it can seem as if all of nature is hard at work while you are relaxing. In the evening the scents are quite different and plants such as evening primrose and woodruff come into their own. By use of grass paths and a chamomile or turf seat you can create a feeling of being in the country even if you are right in the heart of the city. The most important quality to achieve is that of soft femininity. From early times the fragrant herb garden was a place where a lady could escape from the rough world, where lovers could meet in seclusion and where tired minds could find restoration.

If you are planning a garden to supply you with material for pot-pourri then be sure to include a scented geranium such as *Pelargonium*

Right: Old-fashioned roses are essential for the creation of a romantic scented garden, however most of them only flower for a very limited season.

graveolens, P.tomentosum, 'Lady Plymouth' or the lemon-scented *P.citri-odorum.* Although they are quite tender they are vigorous and look splendid when grown in isolation in a pot set in an old chimneypot or on a raised bank. These, together with roses, lavender, marjoram, lemon verbena and bergamot will give you the basis for pot-pourri.

You will need to decide on some arrangement to contain the herbs while at the same time creating the look of an informal setting. Paths are essential, allowing you to pass through the garden and to experience the varied scents. Raised beds sometimes help to enable you to reach plants easily as well as contain them. Utilise all natural features, such as banks or shade-giving trees, and above all keep it simple to begin with. Many annuals will self seed, and weeds should be kept under control, so always arrange your plants so that they can be easily tended and gathered for the home.

Finally, scented gardens are 'secret' gardens and should, if possible, come as a surprise. Entered through a hedge or wall with an attractive gate or soft carpet of chamomile they can always be a place to retreat to or to relax in, where the pace of life slows for a while and your senses are pampered.

Right: The asymmetrical herb garden at Lambeth Palace, London - the residence of the Archbishop of Canterbury - in the process of being replanted. Note the use of curves and circles.

Below: A formal garden created by the author in the south of France, incorporating dwarf box hedging, santolina and rosemary.

The formal garden

The traditional concept of the formal herb garden is that of a geometrically-designed formal shape enclosed by box hedging. In many ways it is the easiest to plan, but it can also be the most complicated in

design. These complicated patterns have evolved as a result of a fascination with shapes and form and embroidery patterns that can be achieved by 'knots'. Knot gardens were designed to be looked down upon, either from an upstairs window or from a raised terrace. By interweaving buxus, cotton lavenders and other hedging herbs such as wall germander, it was possible to construct a pattern incorporating motifs or insignia or plain letters.

In a knot garden the shapes are made by close planting and clipping the hedging plants into shape. Over the years buxus has become the favourite for edgings, and because of its lasting evergreen foliage it makes an ideal plant for year-round interest. In Elizabethan times it was fashionable to put different coloured gravels and pebbles between the patterns, and then as new introductions arrived in England they were placed in these spaces in glorious isolation, to show them off. Simple knot gardens can be planted quite effectively, allowing for the fact that when they die down in the winter the garden takes on a clear formal design highlighted by the frosts and snow.

A simple geometric pattern can be just as effective as a knot, incorporating round or square buxus at the corners and arranging plants architecturally in the larger shaped beds. A central feature such as an

Below: **A perfect cottage garden has to have a cottage! In this Suffolk garden the 16th century building makes an authentic backdrop.**

urn or statue helps to focus the design. The balance is all important and cannot be suitably realised without making a very detailed drawing.

The width of paths in relation to shaped beds is vital and the use of brick and stone is greater enhanced by simple patterns such as basket weave and herringbone designs.

Sometimes the most effective formal gardens use very few varieties of herbs. This is particularly noticeable for example in a garden where the only plantings are cotton lavender and lavender trimmed into square and rounded shapes. The contrast in greys is very pleasing to the eye. I have created a simple formal garden in the south of France with dwarf buxus as edging enclosing cotton lavender (*Santolina chamaecyparissus*) and cotton lavender *S.viridis*, clipping the cotton lavender squarely and the *viridis* into mound shapes rising out of the softer grey cotton lavender. The central feature, an Anduse vase, is surrounded by *Rosmarinus officinalis pyramidalis*, and the paths are lawn. Maintenance is minimal, apart from weeding and two or three cuts a year. However as in all formal gardens you must cut off all the flower heads in order to maintain the formal shape.

The formal garden design, in spite of its mathematical restrictions, can still be flexible in its approach. With modern design techniques, including the use of computers, new and futuristic patterns might be achieved. Pioneers in garden design in this century included such innovative thinkers as Gertrude Jekyll, who wasn't averse to breaking the mould of so-called 'traditional' patterns; using 'keyhole' effects and interlocking circles. The possibilities are there for innovative design, and herbs will always decorate and enhance a good formal pattern.

The cottage herb garden

Cottage gardens were intended to be totally self-sufficient, providing vegetables, herbs and flowers for cutting. They were limited in size to the immediate area around the house and as a result were cultivated intensively. This is why they appear to be a bit of a jumble. But in actual fact they were very carefully planted, allowing for the companion planting to deter pests and increase the yield. The vegetable plot would be planted all around with kitchen herbs. Some, such as chives, would deter carrot fly, while others such as chamomile or yarrow would be there to help increase crop yield.

For many years chamomile has been considered to be a 'doctor' plant, helping to strengthen any plants around it. Yarrow makes a good compost activator and soil improver; pennyroyal keeps ants at bay; and nasturtium acts as a trap for blackfly. Mint, borage and basil are

all good with tomatoes, and mint is also good to plant near cabbages. Tansy, feverfew, wormwood and rue are useful pest repellents, although wormwood should be placed apart from the others and not sited too near roses.

Along the paths in the cottage garden you can plant catmint to provide flower and scent throughout the summer. Winter savory, thyme and hyssop all make good edging borders and pennyroyal, Corsican mint and creeping thymes fill up the cracks in the brickwork. In the herbaceous borders you can mix feverfew, lady's mantle, foxgloves and artemisias with the tall elecampane and fennels among the flowers, allowing chamomile and ladybird poppies to run riot. Borage will self-seed, appearing all over the place each year, and annuals can be sown between rows of vegetables. Roses, pinks, honeysuckle and lilies are perennial favourites in the traditional cottage garden, as are sage, southernwood and all lavenders. Taking into account heights and spread you can fill quite a small area with fragrance and colour that will last throughout the whole of the summer.

The paradise garden

Above: An exhibition paradise garden at Leeds Castle in south-east England. Note the use of wattle surround to isolate important symbolic plants, such as rue in the foreground.

Right: French lavender, *Lavandula stoechas*, is particularly popular with the bees and has the added advantage of flowering early in the year.

The paradise, or love garden dates back to medieval times, particularly the 14th and 15th centuries. This style of garden was the symbolic representation of the art of courtly love, being the pure love of a knight for his lady and incorporating the ideals of chivalry, devotion to the Virgin Mary and Christian beliefs that shaped so much of medieval thought as depicted in art and literature. The ideal location would be a castle courtyard enclosed on all sides by the lady's rooms and chapel. This was her private place of recreation far away from the war-like activities of the rest of the castle, its warriors and knights. The garden was symbolic of her purity, and the only man allowed to penetrate its walls was her husband. The idea originated with the Song of Solomon, in which Solomon recounts the beauties of a perfect sexual union blessed by God.

In a treatise on the soul written in the 4th century, Gregory of Nyssa wrote, 'A garden enclosed is my sister, my bride.' This thinking developed into monastic gardens where, symbolically, Christ was the gardener. Water was introduced in the shape of a well or fountain, which represented Christ's wounds, and in later art the mythical unicorn became the image of Christ's humility and strength. The red rose depicted Christ's blood, shed for mankind, and all these religious images were then woven into the garden style. Every plant in a paradise garden had a symbolic significance.

Tudor times saw more realism and pragmatism - the secular love garden. Here was now a garden to make love in rather than the mystical love garden of chivalry. The paradise garden, like the romantic image of courtly love which inspired it, had dominated European thinking for nearly three hundred years, and its simple concept could and does have an impact today. I have created only one paradise garden, at Leeds Castle in Kent. It was an exhibition garden and existed for its short life in the most perfect setting imaginable. Within the oldest part of the castle is a courtyard adjacent to the queen's bedchamber, with the private chapel and antechambers at the other sides. There is a marble fountain in the centre. All the right ingredients were there.

After turfing over the flagstones we started to experience what it was like to have a little piece of country within the castle walls. A large rue, the 'herb of grace', and spiral buxus to symbolise the unicorn's horn, were placed in wattle surrounds, and two low hedges of santolina and wall germander were set at either end of the rectangular pool in basilica relief. A chamomile seat to one end was flanked by white marguerites and the white flowers of garlic chive. Madonna lilies were put into one corner and the grassy bank under a window planted out with single specimens of rose and white flowers. It wasn't perfect, but it was as near as we could get in early autumn. But the biggest joy was when we turned on the fountain and opened one of the doors from the antechamber and experienced the simplicity of it all. It felt like turning the clock back, and there was a definite spiritual quality to it all.

The bee and butterfly garden

There is an old tradition that if you rub the inside of your beehive with lemon balm then the bees will never leave. Of all the beekeepers I have met none have vouched for this belief, but all are in agreement that balm, among many other herbs, is beneficial to bees and to the quality of honey.

Bees are attracted by colour, particularly blues, pinks and yellows.

Right: By growing herbs in individual pots you can rearrange the plants with the seasons to take advantage of their shapes and colours.

herbs for bees
Thyme
Sage
Rosemary
hyssop
Borage
Winter savory
lemon balm
Lavender French
Bergamot
meadow sweet
evening primrose
chives

So it is essential to have a flowering garden for as long a time as possible. Bees gather nectar from flowers and contrary to belief do not have enormously long tongues, although they do forage from members of the mint family, which have tubular shaped flowers, plants such as thyme, sage, rosemary and, of course, hyssop. Borage is an especial favourite with bees as is winter savory and lemon balm. The ever popular lavender has of course produced honey commercially for years, and bergamot, evening primrose, meadowsweet and chives are a must in a well-stocked bee garden.

It is a good idea to choose a very sheltered corner of the garden to place your hive, and plant a rosemary hedge to protect it. Lemon balm and savory are considered good herbs to have close to the hive, and Eleanor Sinclair Rhodes, the American plantswoman and writer, suggests a hedge of sweet briar.

Early in the year wallflowers provide spring nectar and help the hive off to a good start. Butterflies are attracted to paler colours and to them scent is more important than it is to the bees. The Old English types of lavender and pale pinks such as *Dianthus* 'Doris' are more likely to appeal to them.

If you are going to house bees it is very important that you check their pedigree. I once made the expensive mistake of offering to house a distressed bee colony: it wasn't worth it.

The container herb garden

As far as I'm concerned, plastic is out. Herbs look best in old materials, preferably stone, terracotta or wood. The older the container the better; if you are lucky enough to have antique urns or ancient stone sinks then these are fitting vessels to plant out with herbs. It is an odd fact that these most economical of plants look at their best in expensive antiques. There are, however, excellent stone sinks and terracotta pots on the market that weather well and create the feeling of age quickly.

Although it is possible to put four or five herbs into a sink and two or three into a large pot, the best results come from giving the herb a pot of its own. For interest's sake these can be different shapes and sizes, allowing for an ideal depth of 15cm/6in, except in the case of creeping thymes and chamomiles. You don't just have to use pots - the oddest things can make interesting containers for plants. Not so long ago I saw a garden design using drainage pipes set at different heights which when planted up looked quite good. But if you want to utilise such things as containers do think about what they will look like in the winter; unless you want a view of interesting drain pipes you may have to consider hiding them by placing evergreen perennials all round. However, old chimneypots look good all the time and provide a suitable height for placing a pot in the top, or an excellent container for keeping mint under control, using plenty of broken pots and stones at the bottom for drainage.

An old sink raised up on bricks can often relieve the overall flatness of a flower border, and there is absolutely no reason why you shouldn't mix alpines with small herbs in a sink in a cottage garden setting.

Windowboxes, too often ugly if they are plastic, can be disguised by making a wooden surround and painting this dark green or grey. If you do plant out windowboxes do not be tempted to put in tall fennels or lovage, which need deep containers to accomodate their roots, but confine yourself to pot herbs such as thyme, marjoram, chives, parsley, salad burnet and savory. These will produce a good supply for the year. You will have to re-stock the windowbox annually and feed well during the growing season.

Scented geraniums (pelargoniums) are very rewarding as container herbs and were a great favourite with the Victorians, who filled their porches and front-room windows with enormous specimens. I quite like to add trailing nasturtiums in with the geraniums if the pots are raised up off the ground, so the long-branched stems fall over the edge of the pot and cascade down to the ground.

Hanging baskets can make good containers for herbs but they require a lot of

Below: Standard bay trees can be given more colour with the use of underplanting. These pink petunias are still in their pots, so they can be easily replaced when they fade or begin to look tatty.

attention and watering. The most successful plantings are the simplest, for example lady's mantle mixed with a dark-blue trailing lobelia. Again, do not be tempted to try anything too large as the soil will not be able to provide enough food or room for the roots.

Large evergreens such as buxus and bay are the most common of the container herbs for permanent planting. Buxus should be placed in straight-sided containers to allow the root formation to develop as naturally as possible. It is important to remember that none of these herbs were ever meant to be cultivated anywhere other than in the ground. It is only the ingenuity and techniques that gardeners have developed that make it possible to establish plants in moveable containers.

Buxus and bay can be pruned into many different shapes and used as architectural features. Spirals, obelisks and pyramids are favourite shapes for buxus, whereas ball shapes on bare trunks of bay make pleasing entrances to porches. Buxus can be clipped into low ball shapes, for variation. It has the added advantage of tolerating shade on north-facing terraces. In the late 17th century it was fashionable to have whole armies of gardeners to change the design of pot-grown plants on terraces into a completely different arrangement while the guests dined, creating a new pattern before the diners returned to the garden for the evening's entertainment.

There are some herbs that benefit from being grown in the house, although I would recommend a light airy conservatory for best results. They are, lemon verbena, myrtle, sweet basil and pineapple sage. As mentioned earlier, the scented geraniums will grow well inside the house as well as outside. From bitter experience I find that most culinary herbs hate being inside: they need as much ventilation as possible and very careful watering and feeding. Basil, however, likes nothing better than being placed in a hot steamy bathroom with the sun streaming in on it. There are, thankfully, always exceptions to the rule.

With imagination the grouping of containers with colourful and scented herbs can cheer up any terrace or city balcony. If you have a windy balcony it is best to erect some shelter from heavy breezes, over which you can always grow honeysuckle or jasmine to sweeten the air. If you have a roof garden you can spread the weight of pots by using slatted timber, and although I would like to avoid plastic pots there are now some very fine imitations of terracotta in plastic and these would be less likely to put a hole in your ceiling.

Designing a herb garden

Once you have settled on the style of herb garden, the next step is to draw up a plan. Because the design of your herb garden is important, by putting your ideas down on paper using diagrams and drawings, the layout becomes clear and any problems can be overcome before work begins on the site. The plan doesn't have to be an architect's drawing, but in formal designs this is helpful to anybody laying out the hard landscaping. Measurements are vital to create the right balance;

Right: A simple but effective windowbox of culinary herbs - French tarragon, salad burnet, chives, marjoram and thyme.

and positioning of plants enables you to define shapes and heights. The plan can take the format of a freehand sketch, a detail on graph paper, or a full-blown architect's drawing. All of these depend on the size of your garden. If it is a patch of ground near the kitchen to provide just a few culinary herbs, then there is no need to use graph paper – a simple sketch will do. But if the measurements are crucial, which they often are in a formal design, then it is best to resort to this method and draw a plan to scale. Scale rulers are easy to obtain from good stationery suppliers.

Having chosen the position for your herb garden, draw in the boundaries. This will determine whether or not you need extra hedging, fences or walls. Look beyond the immediate area of the site and see what features affect the location. Then measure up the whole area and, after choosing a scale to suit the size of graph paper, outline the shapes and patterns of the herb beds. It is surprising how often the original idea in your head changes once you commit it to paper.

Now decide on where the paths and paving should go. This may be old brick, paving slabs or shingle. These items are known as 'hard' landscaping features, which also includes walls, fences, trellis, statuary, water features, containers, seating and steps. Work out where all these items are to go and you are then free to include the plants. These are classed as 'soft' features, which is a term covering all plants, trees, shrubs, climbers, hedges and earth features such as banks and mounds. Grass paths and lawns also fall into the 'soft' category. Formal layouts always need low hedges and some focal point such as an urn or a dramatic statue.

When considering a stylised herb garden the theme may dictate the design. A butterfly garden might be arranged in the shape of a butterfly's wings; for a dye garden you could try to re-create a tapestry using a variety of different coloured flowers; and for a biblical or saints' garden you may wish to incorporate a statue of one of the saints.

The Shakespeare garden is less obvious but would be interesting to do. A raised stage could be planted out or beds created using herbs mentioned in his plays.

Making a plan for planting is much simpler once you have created the framework. By measuring the spaces in between low hedges and edgings you can then work out how many herbs you can include in each section. The simple chequerboard design with paving slabs with only one herb to each square makes planning and planting easy, but always be aware of heights, and in such a design either put tall herbs at the centre radiating out in graduated heights, or put tall herbs at the corners. The sheer temptation to cram in as many as possible is overwhelming and I have often added extra plants thinking them small enough for inclusion. But herbs grow quite quickly and reach their optimum heights and widths often in their first season, so be patient and accept the spaces to begin with: they will soon fill in. Use some culinary herbs for borders and allow for shade-lovers and sun-seekers. Mix foliage and flowers to give good variation and always plant some evergreen perennials to offer winter interest.

Once you have made your plan do not panic. You can always move the plants around the following season to achieve the most pleasing effect if things don't turn out exactly as you had hoped.

Designing a knot garden

If you are planning to make a knot garden then you will need to use all your mathematical and design skills. These herb gardens look very like the patterns on oriental and Persian rugs and were particularly popular in the 16th century, although not everybody liked them. Their critics included Francis Bacon, who was quite scathing when he said: 'As for the making of knots, or figures, with divers coloured earths, that they may lie under the windows of the house on that side on which the garden stands, they be but toys: you may see as good sights many times in tarts.'

Bacon's image of laced pastry on jam tarts is very clear and helps us understand how a garden looks in its interwoven design. This is achieved by using different coloured foliage to give the impression of one hedge passing under another. There are some variegated forms of dwarf box if you wish to keep to one type of plant. Alternatively, wall germander, santolina and rock hyssop make good knot hedges. Having chosen your design then try to keep it on a reasonably small scale; 2m/2yd square should be enough to begin with.

However, if you have a flair for draughtmanship then the time taken on an elaborate plan can translate into a fascinating project. An established knot garden is a rare thing, and each and every one is unique and very personal to its creator.

Below: A new herb garden getting nicely established a year after planting. The slow-growing box is doing well but will take a couple more years to join up into a low hedge.

Making a Herb Garden

There is no mystery to creating a herb garden. But there are a few hard and fast rules that will enable you to be successful in your project. Site, sun and well prepared soil are the three most important things to remember. That scrubby bit of badly drained yard at the shady side of the house is not the best place to site a herb garden, in spite of its convenient location. Herbs may sometimes look like weeds but even weeds require some light, and soil that isn't wet and compacted. Look around for that area where the sun shines for at least five hours a day and you will be on your way to finding a good home for your herbs.

We can't all have the perfect soil, but we can improve on what we have, and it doesn't take an awful lot of preparation to do so. Even heavy clay can be made to suit some herbs and in small gardens structures such as a herb spiral can use imported soil.

The site will depend upon the style of your garden. But always be aware of the need to protect the garden from high winds and to trap as much sun as possible. Later I shall suggest different types and varieties of hedges and boundary walls and fences. All of these go to making your garden a more interesting place in which to be. Herb gardens should be places to linger in so benches, seats, arbours and pergolas have an important role to play. You can make turf benches, chamomile seats, rose-covered arbours and covered pergolas to walk through.

The paths can be used as scented walkways or simply as a means of getting from one part of the garden to another, but they must fit in with the general scheme of things and not upset the design balance.. A pathway needs to be functional but must not detract from the overall effect. Never underestimate the need for easy access to herb borders.

Features such as statuary, urns and pots, and topiary can enhance your herb garden, sometimes offering that final touch that makes it individual to you. The decision on what to include is very often an impulsive one inspired by a dream rather than by a planned idea, although sometimes too the object is a long neglected relic that has lain for years waiting for its moment to be resurrected and given pride of place again. One of my favourite seats was one such lost relic, its iron supports left lying where the rotten wooden slats had let them fall, like dead book-ends. With a coat of paint and new slats it made a very comfortable seat again.

Right: A formal box hedge opposite informal edging plants. The White Rose of York, *Rosa alba semiplena,* climbs the old brick wall.

Finally, let your imagination run away with you a little on paper so that you retain a wish yet to be fulfilled for the future. This will keep the garden alive for you as each year goes by.

Choosing your site

You may have already done this before making your plan. If you have, then take the plan to the site and mark out with wooden pegs where the main corners are and see if the alignment is right. By 'pegging out' you can tell immediately if your plan is going to translate successfully or not from paper onto the ground itself.

If you haven't made a plan yet but want to put your herb garden in a particular place - perhaps near to the kitchen, or tucked away somewhere - then go to the site and check the key requirements for good results These are:

Does it get enough sunshine? Five hours is the minimum requirement for good results.

Is there any shade from neighbouring buildings, trees or large shrubs? If there is, can this be incorporated into your design? Obviously a formal garden needs an open setting. But less formal ones can benefit from some shade, particularly if you are growing medicinal herbs, for instance.

Is the soil of reasonable quality, not too dry or too wet? Is it clay or chalk, heavy or light? The presence of nettles can denote good soil, whereas thistles can indicate the need for improving the content.

Will you need to put in hedging or other forms of boundary? After preparing the site this is usually the first job you need to do.

Having satisfied these main criteria then you are ready to take a spade to the soil and begin the preparation for your herb garden.

Preparing the site

Herbs like a well aerated soil allowing their roots to spread easily, and this is best achieved by making the soil crumbly and slightly gritty. It doesn't need to be richly fed as this can make plants weaker and impair their scent. Most plants have originated in the wild and are used to quite rough ground, so don't feel you need to pamper them.

After turning over the soil you will have a good idea whether you have a light or heavy consistency. Drainage is the most important feature and if your soil is heavy wet clay then you will have to spend some time incorporating manure and pea shingle with some sharp sand to help break it up and allow your herb roots to breathe. If the soil is very heavy and will take years to break down then consider creating a herb spiral or growing on raised beds and banks using imported loam mixed with grit. With all the herb gardens I have worked upon I have

Right: A shady herb border containing comfrey, sorrel and sweet woodruff, fronted by silver-grey cotton lavender; all overhung by a tamarix in full flower.

found that the introduction of pea shingle and a little sharp sand has enhanced the growth rate and the herbs have flourished. Manure and compost do help to improve the soil but only add well rotted manure, and apply compost sparingly. I am very fortunate to have a well-balanced soil with plenty of natural grit as it used to be river bed and it therefore drains well too. But every now and then I help it along with a light feed. If you don't have any compost or manure use a little bone meal, which you can buy from a garden centre.

In the impoverished chalk soil of some downland areas the topsoil is minimal and the depth of soil is often limited to only a few centimetres. Raised beds with plenty of mulch, such as homemade compost, can be the answer here. Flints and chalk will always work their way to the surface and the topsoil can dry out very quickly. Do not hope for too neat a garden but do not be deterred by this unforgiving soil; many herbs of the mint, or Labiatae family do quite well in chalk. Examples are: catmint, hyssop, marjoram, rosemary, salad burnet and sage.

If your soil is a heavy acid soil then you will need to add some lime in order to break it down. Only a small quantity is needed and it is best applied in the autumn. If you wish to add manure then wait a while to allow the limestone to work its way in first.

Having then forked over the site you are now ready to plant your hedges or put up your boundary fences, or wall.

Walls and fences

A walled garden is something most of us can only dream about. As well as the aesthetics of plants growing agianst brick, the protection offered and the reflected heat makes a wall an ideal boundary for any herb garden. All the Victorian kitchen gardens for large estates were walled gardens and some still remain. But for us lesser mortals we have to use alternative forms of protection for our plants.

The idea of an enclosed garden isn't something new. It dates back centuries, and many of the old ideas are relevant today. Interwoven wattle fencing secured to stout posts with wire makes an excellent low boundary for attractive climbers. Again, it's the immediate 'old' look that wattle gives which is so attractive.

A low drystone wall can make a useful boundary, allowing you to transform a slope and offer another dimension to the garden. At my first nursery I set a chamomile seat back into a bank, with a drystone wall at either side. Lemon thyme and winter savory with dwarf forms of lavender and hyssop grew happily around the seat. There was enough shade at the foot of the wall to grow Corsican mint and pennyroyal.

Right: A warm red-brick wall offers shelter for comfrey (*Symphytum officinale grandiflorum*) alongside a cut-leaf gold elder 'Sutherland's Gold'.

Overleaf: An ideal formal herb garden using diagonally placed bricks as edging. Such a feature will become more prominent in winter when many of the plants will die back naturally.

Any form of strong wooden fence will support a hop or honeysuckle. Wires can be fixed horizontally to allow for tying in of roses or as a support for hops or clematis. Openwork fencing is often very effective when you can see the herb garden through it: this adds to the effect of an enclosed space.

Tall plants such as angelica, fennel and lovage benefit tremendously from having a backdrop, so it is worth bearing this in mind when creating your boundary. The most important thing to bear in mind is the need for maximum light, so plan the height of your boundaries in keeping with the size of garden.

Paths and paving

Once you have established your boundary then comes the task of 'pegging out' the outline of beds and pathways. This gives you a very precise idea as to how much room you have for edgings and low hedges.

Place pegs of wood at all the corners and tie string between them. Inevitably you are going to compact the soil doing this, so try to mark out your pathways first and lay down boards if you have them.

You will by now have decided on what sort of path you are going to have, but in all cases it is advisable to set a good base of rough rubble or hoggin below a level of sharp sand before laying your bricks or paving. Gravel paths should also have a well broken base of rubble to keep the gravel from sinking into the earth. The better you prepare the rough material the less shingle you require, and you won't end up with a good imitation of a shingle beach, which you have to wade through ankle deep.

In order to enclose and encase your path it is a good idea to set gravel board at the edges, held in by wooden pegs. This is the method I use for what I call a 'living' path, set on sharp sand to allow creeping herbs to be grown in the cracks. This is an altogether pleasing path to make and soon gives the feeling of having been there for a long time. The more permanent path, a favourite with builders, is edged with bricks set on end in a cement mix. However, it can be edged on the garden side with board to allow plants to be grown as close to the path as possible. The average width of a path is either 90cm/39in or 1.2m/4ft for small gardens, although one wide central walkway is more suitable for some designs.

If you can get old bricks, do so. You will always be told of the risk of flaking and cracking in frost, but this just adds to the ageing effect that works so well. The simplest patterns in brick are the best. Tudor pattern, or 'basketweave', and 'herring-bone' are the easiest to lay.

Once you have set your bricks then brush in a mixture of sharp sand and soil into the cracks and sprinkle over with water. This helps to consolidate the mixture and sets the path. Keep adding this mix until the cracks are all filled. Then brush off all the bricks when dry with a stiff brush. If the path is a long one use a spirit level to keep it even, and put boards between the pegs to check your levels.

You can equally well set out stepping stones in soil mixed with gravel in order to plant out a thyme walk. Although this takes a while to establish it makes a very delicate pathway.

Paving stones and cobble stones make good courtyards, allowing for sufficient space in between slabs at varying intervals to plant out herbs. The most effective courtyards are those where herbs have self sown between the cracks and there is a sense of organised chaos about the place.

If you plan on using lawn or chamomile for your paths then it is vital you plant out border plants or low hedges to help define the herb beds.

Below: Brick edging set into concrete acts as a secure border for a well-firmed gravel path. The wattle fence provides a perfect support for climbing plants as well as giving some shelter from the wind.

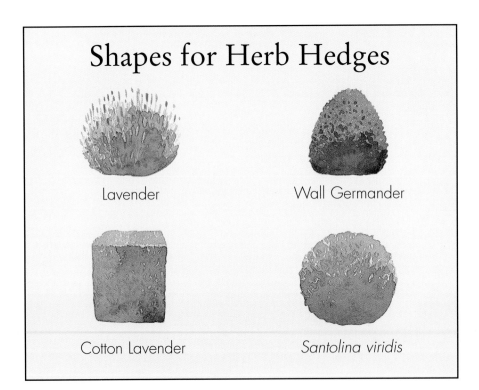

Shapes for Herb Hedges

Lavender

Wall Germander

Cotton Lavender

Santolina viridis

Hedges and edging

Above: Some of these hedging herbs are also suitable for topiary.

Right: Copper-coloured dwarf berberis and grey-green cotton lavender provide a striking contrast in this hedge border, which includes Salix helvetica grown as standards.

Herb hedges are the bones of the garden skeleton. Once you have supplied the structure then you fill in the flesh of the herb beds.

All the hedging plants most suited to edges are shrubby aromatic herbs and evergreens. They can be clipped and cut to shape and have a long lifespan. I have tried rock hyssop as a hedging plant, and although it was highly recommended to me I have found it fails on two counts: it is only semi-evergreen and it needs replacing after four or five years. You need a hedge that will last and look good in the winter months as well. The dark black, leaf-denuded stems of poor old rock hyssop do not make a pleasing sight in the early spring.

My favourites for hedging are: santolina, wall germander, lavender, rosemary and curry plant. The best of all, however, is buxus, or box to give it its common name.

Box hedging is the most formal of herb edgings. It can be trimmed into neat, straight-sided hedges anything up to 1m/3ft in height. There are dwarf varieties which can be set 10-12cm/4-5in apart for an instant hedge. The larger *Buxus sempervirens* needs at least

30cm/12in between the plants to establish a thick hedge over three years. Nothing happens overnight in a garden and you will need some patience with box before you achieve the smooth, manicured lines of an established garden hedge. When choosing your box plants go to a specialist grower who can advise you on the best varieties. There are in fact over 40 different types of box, although the main ones are *B. sempervirens*, *B. rotundifolia* and the dwarf, *B. suffruticosa*. Although box likes moisture it still needs a well aerated soil with the addition of a little leaf mould and peat when planting out. Feed plants in the early spring and don't prune until the frosts are well past in early summer. This allows the new leaf growth to harden off well in time for next winter. Light clipping is possible throughout the summer.

Santolina, or cotton lavender, is particularly effective as an edge for grass paths. The contrast in its light grey colour and the green of the grass makes the hedging stand out and highlights the differences in texture. Cotton lavender can be clipped into straight-sided edges with a flat top in the late spring, and if it gets out of hand during one season then cut it back quite hard in the spring to just above the new growth appearing on lower stems.

Below: **Small irregular-shaped herb beds are enclosed by a mixture of brick and paving.**

Wall germander, which I call poor man's box, makes a good low hedge that can be trimmed into a barrel shape for best effect. The leaves are quite dark. This herb grows on quite quickly and should be set at 10cm/4in apart to create a thick hedge within two years. As with all hedging herbs, do not allow it to flower it you want a good hedge, so trim regularly.

Lavender and curry plant are less easy to shape as they grow in a naturally round habit. Any heavy pruning should be left till the spring and even then you should be careful not to cut back into old wood. It seems a crime not to let lavender flower, so harvest the stalks in late summer and cut all dead stalks off before the winter. But do leave shaping until the following year. All hedging plants can be reared from cuttings, and it is not a bad idea to keep some back in case of loss to any part of the hedge. Then you will have a plant at the same stage of growth with which to replace it. Find another part of the garden where you can keep these stock plants safely.

The upright forms of rosemary such as *R.officinalis* and 'Mrs Jessup's Upright' are particularly suited to large hedges but they do need a sheltered sight to avoid frosting. I have seen rosemary plants clipped savagely but they appeared to suffer little from this and looked very strong and elegant. They can be trimmed throughout the summer but should be left well alone before the first frosts are likely to occur.

In my early experimental days of herb growing I tried rue, hyssop, sage and southernwood as low hedges but found none of them to be satisfactory. You must be able to clip your hedges, and a year-round leaf growth is vital to the whole look of the garden.

Around sunny salad beds a border of chives or garlic works well. Double-flowering chamomile, lady's mantle, winter savory, catmint and dwarf dianthus such as 'Deltoides' - I have used them all as edging plants. The chives are lovely when in flower but look a bit ragged later on, but winter savory gives off the most marvellous scent when you brush past it - and that has to be my favourite.

For mixed vegetable and herb gardens, bricks set at an angle give a neat appearance to the beds and rope terracotta tiles can be quite attractive too.

Seats and arbours

Earth benches were a great favourite with medieval gardeners. They were often brick walls with turf laid in the top. This has given way in modern times to the chamomile seat, of which many types can be made. The easiest to construct is one that is set into a steep bank, as it is not going to be much more than 45cm/18in high unless you want to have your feet dangling in the air. You can build up the front with dry stone and set bricks behind into the soil to create the other three sides. The seat needs to be at least 50cm/20in deep. Make sure the soil drains well and plant out the centre with lawn chamomile, (*Chamaemelum nobile*) 'Treneague', or Roman chamomile. If you want a more solid construction then build a bench surrounded with brick and put plenty of stone and broken crock at the base to assist drainage. Then fill the cavity with earth and plant your herb. You can also try railway sleepers or fill in an old stone seat after removing the top. This type of seat can be planted with low-growing thymes as well; both make soft, sweet-scented places to sit. But do watch out during the flowering season: bees do not take at all kindly to being sat upon.

Below: **Mass plantings of evergreen herbs in these formal semi-circular beds give a solid structure to the design.**

All herb gardens benefit from a seat of one sort or another. You can surround them with sweet-smelling herbs such as lavender, artemisias such as southernwood, pinks and tender perennials such as pineapple

sage and lemon verbena; and you can surround yourself above as well with a shady arbour.

Above: Cotton lavender gives a good splash of colour, but the weight of the flowers opens up the bushes. Also, its pungent scent is not to everyone's liking.

Arbours can serve two main functions; either to conceal the occupant of the seat or to contain the heat of the sun and the scents around you. The view is important, so place your seat where you are going to get the maximum benefit. It is sometimes a good idea to place it directly opposite the entrance to the herb garden so that you can watch for visitors and also make it a focal point. Or you could hide it away in a sunny corner so that it comes as a surprise and offers seclusion as well.

The construction can be quite rustic or as formal as a wrought iron surround. Wooden poles set well into the ground may rot in time but once covered in honeysuckle or jasmine can soon be submerged in scented growth. There are some semi-evergreen honeysuckles, but do make sure they are scented before buying. A briar rose or small flowering climber can be very evocative of the Elizabethan age when it seems everywhere was covered in roses.

Golden hops are quite stunning during the summer and are bold enough to grow over a large pergola. Although hop dies down in the

Above: A rose-covered pergola with catmint borders creates a scented walk within a spacious garden.

early winter once it has produced its heady scented flower cones, it comes again even more strongly the following spring. I don't think clematis should be discounted either just because it's no longer classed as a herb. In particular the *Clematis* 'Tangutica' grows rampantly and produces fairly small but very attractive 'lemon peel' yellow bells in late summer that last well into autumn.

Pergolas are in effect arbours to walk through; as such they can be planted in a similar way. But always think of the view on either side and do not block it out, or you lose the pleasure of the covered walkway.

Lawns and herb banks

To tread on the apple-scented cushion that goes by the name of a chamomile lawn is quite an experience; and if you know how many hours of painstaking work it took to create it you certainly feel you deserve to be delighted. A chamomile lawn conjures up an image of sweet-scented rolling swards of pleasure, but do not be fooled into thinking you can maintain a lawn the size of a tennis court. Think more in terms of a large carpet and then you won't be disappointed.

Start with a small area and then expand into the full area of about 20sq m/66sq ft when you have tested the growth potential. If you have a seat at one end of the lawn then begin your herb lawn around that. Prepare the soil as if you were going to sow a seeded lawn. Remove all weeds and rake the stones off the surface. Tread or roll well and add a little bone meal or fertiliser and leave for a week or two. If the soil is heavy then add a little sharp sand before you roll it. Plant

Below: A decorative seat surrounded by scented herbs such as evening primrose, *Dianthus* 'Doris', Roman chamomile and hyssop.

established chamomile 'Treneague' – or *Anthemis nobilis* if you want flower – quite close together in a criss-cross pattern. For quicker results plant no more than 10cm/4in apart. It will take at least two seasons before you have a decent cushion of chamomile to walk on, and you must remove all weeds before they become established. Chamomile spreads from its centre and often dies down at the centre having sent out its runners. So be prepared to fill in these gaps with some of the offshoots as and when they appear. 'Treneague' needs no more than a very light trim in the summer, but the Roman chamomile *Anthemis nobilis* will need to be cut with shears on a regular basis during the growing season. But do not be downhearted by the threat of high maintenance. Once established, you will only have to keep an eye out for rogue weeks. If you have the time and patience you can create a lush green carpet to give you pleasure all summer through.

You can also make lawns from creeping thymes using the same technique, although I like to put plenty of grit at the surface to allow the plants to grip onto something as they spread their rooting stems outwards. You can create patterns with the different colours and allow for some to follow on from others in the flowering season. Thyme's also useful for filling in gaps that often occur in a chamomile lawn.

I had a herb garden once with quite a steep bank which was south-facing and had a variety of light and shade, the result of a large bay tree on my side and the neighbour's trees on the other side. I was amazed by the angelica which grew at the top of the bank; it was so large it gave the impression of a tree. Comfrey grew in the shade of the bay tree with woodruff and foxgloves on the other side in the shade of the trees. However, it also struck me that not all the herbs did well on that bank and it was some time before I realised that drainage was the problem. If you consider that dry herbs can grow at the top of the bank while moisture-loving herbs such as chives need to go to the bottom, then you begin to create something like a wild habitat, where St John's wort, alpine strawberry and cowslips find their own growing areas. By moving them around I began to discover their natural needs, and so it was that I came to discover the herb spiral.

The herb spiral

Right: Pergolas need not be elaborate structures to be effective: here a simple wooden one is almost swamped by a climbing rose, golden hops and intertwined ivies.

In order to make as near perfect an 'eco-system' for culinary herbs as possible, the science of permaculture has devised the 'herb spiral'. Permaculture is an environmentally friendly system using improvisation and the resources available to develop organic ways of cultivation. If herbs are given their natural environment they will be more resistant to

pest and disease and need little help from artificial feeds and additives. The herb spiral creates the best drainage and light principles for a variety of culinary herbs, so providing a suitable herb garden that requires the minimum maintenance and yet gives the maximum yield. Plants at the top of the spiral are in drier soil than those at the bottom. So herbs such as rosemary can get the most light with less moisture, whereas mint and chives can gain shade from the walls and mositure at the bottom of the spiral. Watering can be carried out from the top and run down to the damper parts below.

If you also consider that it only takes up an area about 1.5m/5ft across and less than 100cm/39in high it is an ideal small garden to place near the kitchen. It can be constructed with around 100 bricks or dry stone walling and is remarkably easy to build. If you wish you can place a small plastic-lined pool at the base in which to grow watercress (Rorippa nasturtium-aquaticum).

Left: Paths should lead to a focal point - such as this distant fountain at Hollington Herb Nursery in Berkshire.

Below: The herb spiral displays all your culinary herbs in an unusual arrangement, offering ideal light, shade and drainage conditions. Bricks or stones can be set to form a spiral without any need for mortar or cement. Rosemary, which prefers dry conditions, can be planted at the top and moisture-loving herbs such as chives and garlic at the bottom.

A Herb Spiral

Growing Herbs

Herbs are grown in three different ways: from seed, from cuttings and by root division. All these methods are easy to do; you need only follow a few simple guidelines to achieve success. You can help yourself enormously by using the right equipment as this will maximise your results. There are some excellent proprietary composts on the market for seeds and seedlings and you can also make up your own mix if you so wish. Here then is a list of items you need for propagating:

- Seed or plug trays
- A garden sieve
- A small dibber (for making holes)
- A good sharp knife (for cuttings)
- Plant labels
- Indelible pens, or pencil
- Potting tray
- Glass to cover seeds
- Good quality compost for seeds and cuttings
- Small pots for seedlings and cuttings
- Spray or watering can with fine rose
- Hormone rooting compound

Growing from seed

Generally, herbs grown from seed tend to be annuals or biennials. However, there are some perennials such as chives, marjoram and thyme that can be grown from seed, although they do seem to take a long time.

Spring is the busiest seed-sowing season for herbs like chervil, dill, catmint, borage, chamomile, fennel, hyssop, lemon balm, marjoram, meadowsweet, parsley, rocket, salad burnet, summer savory and thymes. I like to wait until the warm days of late spring before sowing basil and coriander.

Spring sowings can be done in seed trays and started off indoors under glass. The ideal place, of course, is a greenhouse, although a sunny window sill, an airing cupboard or conservatory will do just as well in the early stages. But do make certain you keep a constant eye on your sowings at all times.

Either fill a seed tray or plug tray with seed compost. Plug trays are much easier to get now, and give you the chance to produce rooted

Right: The border in early spring should be planned to show a good selection of contrasting leaf-shapes and flower colour.

Annual Spring herbs
Chervil
dill
catmint
borage
chamomile
fennel
hyssop
lemon balm
marjoram
meadowsweet
parsley
Salad burnet
Summer Savory
Thyme

seedlings separated from each other and therefore less likely to suffer from root disturbance when potted on. Seed compost can be bought ready mixed or you can make your own with a mix of peat and sharp sand, in a ratio of 70 per cent peat to 30 per cent sand. Or you can mix equal portions of peat and well composted forest bark. If you are unhappy about using peat, then there are some good peat substitutes, for example coir fibre, but I find they tend to dry out rather more quickly. If peat comes from a well-managed peat bog, then there is no reason why the land should be depleted. There have been, in addition, large tracts of peat bog discovered in Russia, and peat from there is being exported world-wide. Another method is to use ordinary garden soil, sterilise it and then mix it with some sharp sand.

Gently firm the compost down. In a seed tray, you can use the base of a flowerpot to do this; with a plug tray you can tap the whole tray down on an even surface. This will settle the compost in the compartments. Sow your seeds thinly and lightly cover with some sieved compost. If your seeds are very small, only use a light covering. Water with a fine rose, but only just enough to dampen the soil: you don't want to soak the compost completely.

Cover the seed trays with glass to keep in the moisture and place newspaper over the glass to exclude the light while the seeds germinate. Some seed trays come with a clear lid, in which case you need only cover this with newspaper.

Put your trays in a warm place to bring the seeds on. Cover with a sheet of glass and place a piece of newspaper on top to keep out the light. Germination can take as little as five days or, in the case of parsley, anything up to two or three weeks, so keep checking the trays daily for moisture retention and the first sign of the seedlings appearing. As soon as the seedlings show, remove the glass and the newspaper and place in a light and airy place so that you encourage strong, straight seedlings to develop.

Pricking out

If you are using plug trays you will need to reduce the seedlings to one per plug. If you are using seed trays you will have to 'prick out' the

Below: The greenhouse is ideal for housing a selection of herbs which have been grown on from cuttings. These young plants are now strong enough to be gently hardened off and planted outside.

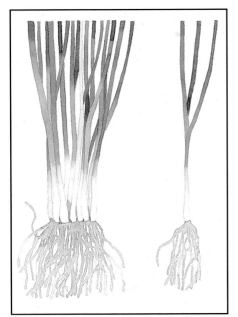

Above: Chives can be propagated in early spring by gently prising apart the bulblets into smaller clumps.

Right: Some plants, such as lovage can be multiplied by root division using a sharp knife.

Far right: Lovage will readily produce new growth from all parts of its root.

overcrowded young seedlings, taking care to moisten the soil first and isolate each chosen seedling without disturbing its roots. This is a labour of love. But when you have divided all your seedlings into well separated rows it is very satisfying. Give yourself plenty of time to do this task and all will be well.

If the danger of heavy frosts has passed and the soil is easily worked into a fine tilth, then you can sow seeds outdoors. Rake the soil well and make a shallow drill with a stick or edge of the rake. Moisten the bottom of the drill and sow the seeds thinly. Lightly cover the seeds with soil and then cover with a cloche, if you have one. Don't worry if you haven't, the seeds will just take a little longer to germinate.

Always mark your rows clearly with indelible pen on a good-sized label. Even with your seed trays it helps to mark them in some way in case you get into a muddle after sowing.

Keep seedlings moist with a fine spray but be careful not to overwater at this early stage. Keep a watch at this time of the year for the plants that have self-seeded from last season. Dill, borage, feverfew, parsley, fennel and chervil are all self-seeders.

Growing on

Once your seedlings have made a good root system and grown more than two leaves you can pot them on. With plugs this is a relatively easy process, but either way you need to be patient and careful in your task. Having first watered your seedlings well, prise them gently out of the compost and transplant them into a potting compost mixture.

Fill your flowerpots in advance. Small pots are best at this stage, as they allow the roots to hit the sides of the pots quickly and so develop a strong root system. You can buy very good multi-purpose potting composts or make your own mix, remembering to include a fertiliser and vermiculite to help aerate the soil. In all good mixes you need loam, peat, grit, vermiculite, sharp sand and fertiliser. You can use short- or long-term fertilisers, but if you use short term ones you will need to add a liquid feed after 12 weeks.

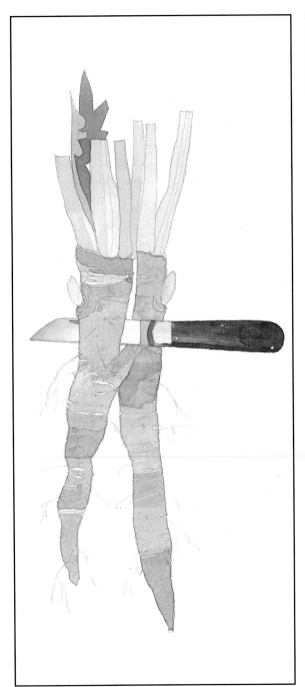

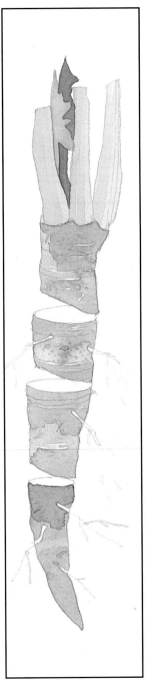

Using your dibber, make a hole large enough to take the seedling, and, lifting by a leaf, gently place the seedling into the pot and firm lightly around it. It is necessary to avoid picking up seedlings by their stems as this can damage the plant and retard its growth.

I like to grow my young seedlings in the greenhouse to begin with. You can use a sunny windowsill if you don't have a greenhouse, but keep turning the plant to encourage it to grow straight up. All-round light guarantees a straight strong young plant. I place the pots on pea shingle to allow them to drain easily, but there are many forms of water-absorbing matting to put on greenhouse shelves, which help to retain moisture at the roots. Watering is important at this stage. Young plants need moisture on a regular basis, but do not like getting their feet too wet. If you water from above and use a spray mist for the leaves this will provide all the moisture they need.

After two or three weeks you will need to harden the young plants off. Take them from the greenhouse as the days warm up and put them in a sheltered, airy place, continue to water and, if necessary, feed lightly. You will notice them strengthen quite quickly and very soon they will be ready to plant out in the garden.

At the planting-out stage herbs can look quite small, so check the size and spread of your plants beforehand. Make sure the soil is well turned and able to drain freely. Water in the young plants using a watering can with a fine rose spray attachment, and then simply wait for them to grow. You will be surprised at just how quickly they come along.

Root division

Root division serves two important functions. It is an easy way to increase herbs such as chives and comfrey, and it helps to check the invasiveness of prolific spreading herbs such as mint.

With thick-rooted plants, for example comfrey and lovage, it is nec-essary to use a sharp knife to cut the roots apart. This is best done in the spring when the plant is still dormant, although you can divide in late autumn as well. After digging up the herb, take it to a firm table or bench to do any cutting. Then replant the divided sections and firm in well.

Right: Always take soft-wood cuttings from just below a leaf node. Place it in a polythene bag tied securely at the top. This will ensure that the cutting is as fresh as possible when you pot it up.

Chives can be divided in late winter just as the green spears start to show above ground. Dig up the clumps and gently prise the bulblets apart, replanting only five or six together and spacing 10-15cm/4-6 in apart. This way you can create a border with only a few clumps. Mint can be dug up in the spring and divided into roots of only

15cm/6in each. Discard and destroy all unwanted roots and firm those roots you are keeping into the soil, either in new beds or pots.

Other perennials can be divided with a fork or pulled apart. Lady's mantle and marjoram are good examples with which you can use this method. Woodruff and creeping thymes sometimes divide best in late summer while tarragon, meadowsweet and valerian can happily be divided in the early autumn.

Softwood cuttings

You can use the same compost for cuttings that you used for seeds, and plug trays make excellent containers for easy cultivation. Softwood cuttings, as the name implies, are soft top shoots of shrubby, mostly aromatic herbs and are best taken in late spring and early summer. Typical plants are: santolina, curry plant, lavender, sage, rosemary and the artemisias.

Take the tip of a vigorous shoot with no flowers and cut it off about 10cm/4in from the top. Reduce this by half and remove the lower leaves. Dip the base in hormone rooting compound (although I find this is not particularly necessary with soft herbs) and firm into the compost. For rosemary and lavender add a little more sharp sand to the mix, as it helps these plants to root more vigorously.

Water the cuttings well and place in a shady place outdoors, in a cold greenhouse or on a shady windowsill. Some people suggest you create a moist climate for your cuttings by placing a plastic bag over your pots with small canes to keep the plastic away from the leaves. This can speed up the process, but I have always found it difficult to keep in a lasting shape and the cuttings quite often get too wet and dampen off. This may, of course, be my own ineptitude, but the success rate of more open methods

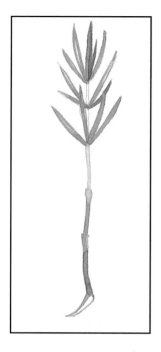

seems to confirm my belief that a good idea has been allowed to develop too readily, causing great disappointment when cuttings fail. Trial and error will determine the best way for you.

Another method, which I have found is successful with rosemary, is to take quite large cuttings and press them into the ground underneath the mother plant. The natural shade and suitable soil help the shoots to root quite easily.

Semi-hardwood cuttings

Semi-hardwood cuttings are taken in late summer and hardwood in the autumn. Suitable herbs are hyssop, lemon verbena, scented geranium, rosemary, rue, wall germander and thyme. These shoots are longer than softwood cuttings and more developed. If you can remove the shoot taking a little of the bark with it then this is known as a 'heel', and helps to make the cutting take more easily. Use a similar compost to the softwood cutting compost and add a little more sharp sand to the mixture. Place cuttings in pots, singly, in a shady area and allow to root before removing to a lighter place and the planting out. All cuttings need light and air once the new shoots begin to appear.

Above: A rosemary cutting.
Below: Layering rosemary with a peg.
Right: 'Mounding up' an old sage bush.

Maintaining a Herb Garden

By using the information below as a guide to the seasonal care of your herbs you can minimise problems and make the most effective use of your time.

Spring

Spring is the busiest time of the herb year. I prefer to do all hard pruning after the worst of the frosts are over. Tall growth on hyssop, germander, marjoram, santolina, southernwood and so on have protected them from the worst effects of snow and ice. Now you need to encourage the new growth coming from the base of the plant, and the lower stems. Some herbs, such as lavender, should only be cut back to last year's new growth. Avoid cutting back into old wood. However, the artemisias in particular, as well as rue, need a hard prune – only a few centimetres above the soil – to promote new strong shoots. For a few weeks they will look bare and forlorn. No one likes to look at bare brown stems, but this is necessary if you are going to enjoy full, well-shaped bushes in the summer.

Using a sharp pair of secateurs, cut back old growth and dead flowering stems left over from the autumn. This now gives you the chance to fork over the soil around the shrubby herbs and add a little bone meal or well-rotted compost. Remember not to overdo it: too much feeding can be just as bad as too little. Herbs need some food, but not an orgy of muck. Save that for the roses.

The benefit of growing old fashioned rose varieties such as the Apothecary Rose is that they need very little pruning. Take off any fruit left over from last year and just clip the tips to shape the bush. Lightly fork all around and give the bushes a feed with well-rotted manure or specialist rose feed. Old fashioned roses are quite delicate and need careful handling – their thorns are the sharpest you are likely to encounter.

Sage plants look worse than any other herb after the winter. Do not be disheartened by this. Wait until late spring and then cut hard back to the new growth which appears from the bottom of the woody stems. To encourage these you can cut the tips off in mid-spring and propagate cuttings from them.

This is an exciting time of year for really keen gardeners who are watching for new shoots to emerge, and seeing which plants have self-seeded. It is a also a good time to observe patiently the rates of growth

Right: By late summer the chives have long since lost their flower-heads, and others such as *Santolina* 'Lemon Queen', *Rosa* 'Alberic Barbier' and hyssop, show the benefit of good pruning.

and the time it takes for some plants, such as evening primrose, to appear. Do take care, therefore, not to tread the soil too much, as you could be destroying newly germinated seeds. There are some herbs, including feverfew, that self-seed far too readily and can take over if allowed to do so. Be bold and remove anything you don't want. I know it seems wicked to throw away any plant, but sometimes it is necessary to be ruthless. I have seen a number of jungles, which are the result of sentimental gardeners.

Early spring is an ideal time to divide chives and lift mint for replanting. Chives can be lifted at the first sign of their reappearance and split up for stronger growth in the summer. Mint needs to be lifted in order to check its invasiveness, but also because it is a traveller and therefore is prone to die off at its original planting place. Dig up the roots that have developed over the winter and cut the new, strong roots (which have tiny fibrous root hairs showing) into short lengths. Return these to the soil with a little compost and just press them into the surface. Space each one a little distance apart and water in.

Above: A splendid spiral topiaried *Cupressus* 'Goldcrest' in a formal box parterre with terracotta pots containing young plants.

Once you have done all the spring cleaning and trimming keep an eye on the weather. In a very dry spring, you must give a light sprinkling of water to encourage the growing process. If there is reasonable moisture, then apply a light foliar or root feed.

Container-grown plants need a great deal of attention at this time of year. That thyme plant, for instance, that did very well in its small pot last year now needs to be grown on in a larger pot. All container-grown herbs can quickly become 'pot-bound'. A new lease of life in fresh compost and with room for the roots to spread can work wonders for an ailing plant, tired after the winter and in need of nourishment.

All windowboxes should be replanted and large container plants such as bay and box will need a liquid feed from now on as well as regular watering. Check for any first signs of aphid and spray with a good soap-based pesticide.

Summer

Dead-head all roses as they die off to encourage new buds to flower.

This is the season of salads, and your herb garden will be looking its best between early summer and the onset of autumn. Keep cutting back all vigorous growing herbs such as sorrel, lovage, mint, fennels, and lemon balm and use chives, parsley, basil, dill, rocket and so on.

Now is also the time to begin to harvest your herbs for drying. The simple rule that applies to harvesting any herb is, only harvest on a dry day, and even then wait until the dew has dried on its leaves and just before the sun starts to warm it enough to denude it of essential oils. The most potent time for herbs is just before they come into flower.

Most of the Labiatea family and the artemisias produce oil from tiny glands in the leaves. By waiting until the plant is just about to flower you can catch it at its best.

Late summer sees seed heads appearing and these will need to be harvested for next year's seeds and for the kitchen.Continue to feed windowboxes every week, and water hanging baskets daily. If the weather is very hot and dry you may need to water well twice a day

Weeding is a chore, but a necessary one, as grasses can quickly grow up through your herbs and become entangled in the roots, making it very difficult to remove them the following year. Young thyme seedlings may appear at any time from late spring through summer, and can usefully be potted on to fill any gaps evident in the autumn.

From early summer you can trim and prune bay and box plants. Topiary can be shaped and fed with a good foliar feed, hedges kept in trim and flower heads cut off if you wish to keep the tight shape. Later into the summer a mulch can be beneficial for all woody-stemmed herbs as they retain moisture and are prepared for the cold autumn nights.

Below: The 'Apothecary Rose', *Rosa gallicia officinalis,* is one of the oldest roses in cultivation. Throughout June it produces beautiful but delicate flowers that drop at the slightest touch. It is at this stage that they are ripe for harvesting for potpourri and medicinal tinctures.

Autumn

Autumn is the time to harvest roots. These include angelica, elecampane, marshmallow, horseradish, chicory and comfrey. Comfrey can also be divided, although I prefer to do this in the spring. Flowerheads need to be cut off as they die, and you should cut back lemon balm and evening primrose. Lavender spikes should be cut off, but do not be tempted to prune lavender until the following year. Continue to mulch and take up half-hardy perennials such as lemon

verbena, scented geraniums, myrtle (if outdoors), pineapple sage, tricolor sage and basil. You will need to pot them up so they are ready to bring into the house or greenhouse where they will be protected from frosts.

If you haven't already done so in late summer, take cuttings from the scented geraniums and trim back pineapple sage and lemon verbena.

Now is the time to stop feeding and allow your herbs to rest in order to prepare for the dormant period of winter. Early autumn is a particularly busy time for those who pickle and make jams and jellies, chutneys and vinegars, all of which will benefit from the adddition of herbs in some way.

Winter

Apart from the woody-stemmed, shrub-like herbs such as rosemary, thyme, marjoram, winter savory, hyssop and so on, many herbs die down in the winter and disappear completely until the following spring. The woody herbs need protection from severe weather with a dressing of leaf mould or well-composted forest bark. However, remember that these mulches should not be left around the plants for too long the following spring, as otherwise they will trap too much moisture around the herbs.

It is a good idea to mark where French tarragon, chives and mint are growing, so that you are not too alarmed by the gaps they will leave during the long winter months.

In exposed areas it is essential to protect herbs from cold winds. Screening and spun coverings help, if they are put over the plants in extremely cold weather. Bay, unless it is near the warmth of the house, will need to be brought inside, although I have found bay trees in this country to be remarkable resilient, recovering their leaf if given the chance and responding to clipping again the following summer.

You are bound to experience some losses; sometimes, as a result of very damp winters. Treat this philosophically and enjoy the fruits of your summer labours with dried herbs and pot-pourri around the winter fires.

Right: The evidence of late frost damage is clear on these box hedges. If you live in an area prone to late frosts, it is advisable to trim your hedges into rounded shapes during the summer, thereby avoiding the possibility of excess water settling on them and causing winter damage.

Index